love
Pain

Sea of
Strangers

Also by Lang Leav

Sea of Strangers

Poetry & Prose

LANG LEAV

Andrews McMeel
PUBLISHING®

Andrews McMeel Publishing
a division of Andrews McMeel Universal
1130 Walnut Street, Kansas City, Missouri 64106

www.andrewsmcmeel.com

www.langleav.com

18 19 20 21 22 RR2 10 9 8 7 6 5 4

ISBN: 978-1-4494-8989-2

Library of Congress Control Number: 2017959243

ATTENTION: SCHOOLS AND BUSINESSES
Andrews McMeel books are available at quantity
discounts with bulk purchase for educational, business, or
sales promotional use. For information, please e-mail the
Andrews McMeel Publishing Special Sales Department:
specialsales@amuniversal.com.

For Michael
You, me, and the sea.

Introduction

It has been almost a decade since I wrote the poem *Sea of Strangers*. I still remember that moment with great clarity. I was coming to the end of a difficult period in my life, though when the end isn't in plain sight, you don't realize how close you are.

I was drifting to sleep when the poem hit me like a lightning bolt. I sat up and grabbed my pen and notebook. My hand could hardly keep up with the words that were rushing into my mind. When the poem was down on paper, my eyes flooded with tears. I felt a powerful sense of relief, one I can't explain even to this day.

I had no way of knowing, when I was sitting alone in that tiny bedroom, that in just a few short months, I would meet the love of my life: a man who lived across the ocean from me, in a little house by the sea. I didn't know I would cross that ocean to be with him, that waiting for me on the other side was a life I'd always longed for but never expected to find.

The way the poem *Sea of Strangers* came to me and what transpired afterward is a testament to the power of words. I know with all my heart those words were like a compass that led me here, and I hope they will lead you somewhere beautiful too.

Sea of Strangers

In a sea of strangers,
    you've longed to know me.
    Your life spent sailing
    to my shores.

The arms that yearn
    to someday hold me,
    will ache beneath
    the heavy oars.

Please take your time
    and take it slowly;
    as all you do
    will run its course.

And nothing else
    can take what only—
    was always meant
    as solely yours.

Take things as you
see it..

New Beginnings

If I have learned anything this year, it's that I won't ever be ready for what life throws at me. I will never be adequately prepared. I won't have the right words when it counts for something. I won't know the right answer when fate itself is staring me down.

I've learned I can go on waiting for something, sustained by hope and nothing more, or I can put it to one side and shrug my shoulders. Bravely accept the fact that I can't keep my heart safe any more than I can stop love from taking everything from me.

I have learned to stop saying yes when I don't mean it— to live as authentically as I know how. To allow the tips of my fingers to skirt the darkness, as long as I remember to keep my eyes fixed on the light. And as one door opens and another closes, I will move forward with the knowledge that unlike so many others, I have another year ahead of me— another shot at making it all the way around the sun, and a chance to get it right this time 'round.

Keys to the Kingdom

If a boy asks you for your name, don't give it to him. He will say it back to you in a voice like gravel and honey, and you will crave his hands all rough and sweet. But you're not the kind of girl who builds her house from sticks; you are a fortress, stubborn and strong. Do not give away the keys to the kingdom to anyone less than a king.

You Had Me Once

You had me once—
    wild and willing;
    you wanted a lover
    who took you to the edge.

Wasn't it I—
    who gave you that feeling?
    A love that danced
    upon a ledge.

Then came another
    who offered you safety—
    and you chose to be
    with her instead.

Hi Stranger

Contentment

There was a time when I thought I wanted more. When I saw the sky as a soaring highway and the world as one big carousel. But those yearnings have grown so distant, ebbed so far away from me, they feel as though they belong to someone else. All I want now is a rainy day, a roaring fire, you and I talking about how quickly the time has gone.

Hey..

Witness

It is the mark of a great poet to write words that feel as though they have stood witness to your most intimate memory of love.

Reclaiming the Sky

Ask the sun to relinquish
      the sky to the moon.

Tell the moon to rise
      with a fierce
      unyielding vengeance.

Remind her it is now
      her time to glow.

Moving On

Leave him, let him go. Don't be the crazy ex-girlfriend or the shoulder to cry on. You're more than just an ego boost, a story he can tell someone he's trying to impress. Just walk away with your head held high and don't give him another second of your time. I know you love him so much that every step is killing you. But this is the moment you'll always look back on as the day you put yourself first. Go and make something beautiful of your life and I promise you, one day you'll forget he was ever there.

Shelter

My father was a house,
my mother was a home.

We Never Broke Up

We never broke up. I am on my second cup of coffee and you're just waking up. The sun is streaming through the curtains and I go to kiss your back.

We never broke up. You find me on the bathroom floor again after a bad day. You pick me up and we talk it through. You tell me nothing is ever as bad as it seems. Not when we have each other.

We never broke up. It is two in the morning and we're laughing so much, it hurts. We keep telling each other to go to sleep, but neither one of us does. I was so happy— I could have died that night. Sometimes I wish I had.

We never broke up. Only, we did. As I lie awake wishing, willing you here. Dreaming of the day you're in my arms again, asking me why did we ever break up.

Happiness

- Sun/moon/stars
- Believing other life is out there
- feeling
- love
- flowers
- friends/family
- Adventures
- Books
- Music (new/old)
- fires
- expressing yourself
- feeling alone then remembering you aren't!
- Jokes
- poems!
- Thoughts
- pictures
- memories
- Candles

Into Existence

If you wrote a line about me, it could never be false. Even if it is. Don't you see? You are writing me into existence, so please be careful with your words.

wanting/needing something but not knowing what!

Broken

They put me in a gown and sat me in a chair and a man in a white coat showed me picture card after card and said *tell me the first thing that comes to your mind*.

First he showed me a china plate and I said, *hunger.*

Then he showed me a dead bird and I said, *fallen.*

Then he showed a picture of you.

I closed my eyes and said, *broken.*

Darts on a Board

I don't know if it was me or her or the one who came before that. What did it matter? We were all just darts on a board, wishing we had hit the bull's-eye.

The Fisherman

I spend a lot of time thinking, maybe a little too much, about things that have been. Like when we first met and I told you someday, I would marry a fisherman and live by the sea. Then as we began to fall in love, that throwaway comment grew in significance.

Whereas you, on the other hand, are always thinking, *what if?* Spinning these wild hypotheticals that are sometimes sad, other times hilarious. Often, I wonder if we are living in one of them. But then, I don't think it's possible—even for you—to conjure something up this perfect.

And that is our main point of difference. I will keep mining ground we've covered to see if there is anything worth salvaging, and you will always be looking for new territory to explore. But there will be times when we switch, when you will be behind that metal detector, and I will be standing at the helm.

So we'll always be okay. I'm certain of it because this, right here with you, is everything I have ever wanted. You're my fisherman.

. . . .

I love it.

The honesty and insight make this story so precious.

> *I will keep mining ground we've covered to see if there is anything worth salvaging, and you will always be looking for new territory to explore. But there will be times when we switch, where you will be behind that metal detector, and I will be standing at the helm.*

I am your fisherman. Come live with me by the sea.

Where It Hurts

There are days when the melancholy settles on you like a sudden change in weather. The kind of sadness that is intangible. Like the presence of an ache where you can't pinpoint exactly where it hurts, you just know it does.

¿ *An Impossible Ideal* ?

Men don't compare us
with other women.
They compare us
to an ideal.

Take Back Your Power

Greet the world with no expectation.
Love as though you have never been hurt or betrayed.
Let go of the ones who take so much from you
yet offer nothing in return.

This is how you take back your power.

Anything for Love

Fear isn't a reason when it comes to love—it's an excuse. Anyone who has ever been in love will tell you that. When it happens, you don't think about the consequences. You'd turn your life upside down to be with that person. You'd do anything for them.

By the Sea

They say that those who live by the ocean are waiting for something. Someone must have decided long ago to put me by the sea. To live each moment by the light of the stars.

I cross off days in the calendar, although it seems inconsequential. In a blink of an eye, an hour can stretch into years. And I think my love has forgotten me. As I am caught somewhere between the sky and water, like the moon, waxing and waning, tending the tides.

Read!

The Things She Asked

That was what got to her the most. The things she asked for were so infinitesimally small, she felt as though she shouldn't have had to ask.

High Tide

Are you somewhere looking at the sea, my love?
    You loved to watch the tide come in.
    Loved the fullness of it.
    Said that's how your heart was
    when I smiled. I was angry once
    about how much you loved my smile.

Some days it felt like a burden, to smile for you.
    To keep the lines of worry
    from etching into your forehead.

You said I was the girl who couldn't decide
    between the ocean and the shore.
    Said the only way to make me fall in love
    with the present was to turn it into my past.

Have You?

After all these years without you, I haven't reconciled this pain. I have yet to make peace with it.

I don't even know where to begin.

They promised me that time would fix it, but seeing you again takes me right back to yesterday.

And every day from then to now, subsisting on the lies I tell myself when the truth is, I can't let go, I haven't let go.

Have you?

Falling into You

It was so easy falling into you again, like losing my place in a book and then retracing my steps back into the past, to find the part in the story I left off.

A Wild Goose Chase

The things I sought
    could not be bought,
    nor do I know
    where to find them.

All his thoughts,
    the ideas they court,
    and if I am inside them.

Strength

Don't let them tell you that your pain should be confined to the past, that it bears no relevance to the present. Your pain is part of who you are.

They don't know how strong that makes you.

Read♡

Writing

There is one thing you should know about writing. It will inevitably lead you to dark places as you cannot write authentically about something unless you have lived it. However, you should always bear in mind that you are only a tourist and must always remain one. You were blessed with the gift of words, in order to bring a voice to suffering. But do not be too indulgent despite how addictive sadness can be, how easy it is to get lost down the path of self-destruction. You must emerge from adversity, scathed but victorious to tell your story and, in turn, light the way for others.

Forever on My Mind

I thought of you with
    my heart already broken;
    I thought of you
    as it was breaking again.

I think of you now,
    as I am healing.
    With somebody new—
    I'll think of you then.

Back There Again

I know he found you and brought you out of the darkness.
But don't forget he put you back there again.

With Anyone Else

You came into my life and made everything else feel like a rehearsal. Love always came to me as a question, but with you, it felt like an answer. I didn't know I had put up walls until you brought them crashing down. I couldn't figure out why love was different with you until I realized it hadn't been love with anyone else.

From Everyone

When you don't have the whole attention of *someone*,
you find yourself begging for it from *everyone*.

"You were like my candle.
The flame that didn't stop.
I started, you never stopped.
Always on my command."

"Soft hands, soft lips, easy going."

"So close, yet so far. how i view
life on the stars."

"I read you like a poem.
Always soft words; hard to
read."

"you, oh you. i've never adored
anything else more then you."

"i loved you more than i loved
myself. i hate you more then
i hate myself."

the first night we talked, we
talked for hours. I had you
and the stars around us.
i can never read you. you
are harder

My Place in the Universe to read
than a poem

I feel my life culminating to a point, the delicate threads of
my existence joining to form a tapestry. The events up until
the present that had seemed of no particular significance,
now imbued with a deeper, darker meaning.

I can see it so clearly—the greater plan. I understand that I
am both the architect and tenant of my destruction. I can feel
it so acutely like an ache in my chest, knowing ultimately
that I am locked into a chain of events that I cannot stop,
an outcome I cannot alter, feeling at once helpless yet
hopelessly awed by the power of my part in this beautiful,
brutal expression of the Universe.

a few weeks go by, your
still around. You compared
me to cocaine.. you meant
it in a good way, i took
it in both ways.. please dont
make me addicted to you, i
dont want to get hurt. i guess
if youre the one hurting
me, it'll be worth it..

one heart ach, one heart
break. please patch me back
up before all of me breaks.

to me, to you
my love,
my skin,
my body,
my mind,
take it all, all of me.
leave me nothing but
your love behind.

Meant to Be

If they were meant to be in your life, nothing could ever make them leave. If they weren't, nothing in the world could make them stay.

please be meant to be.
i want you to be more
than anything else. i want
you more than you
want me, i just hope
you never realize it.
i hope you leave me
before i get to attached.
i'd never leave you, i like
you to much."

Shield You

Who are the ones who are saying those things about you? What right do they have to pass judgment on your gift? Don't you know how you emanate light? So bright they can't look away.

Don't you know since the dawn of time, poetry has been used to shield you from those who mean to do you harm? The greatest power lies in our words, and these are the ones I have written to keep you safe.

Memories Lost

If I could, I would erase myself from your memory.
You would lose all recollection of loving me.

You won't remember why you stopped.

September Love

How many years must we put between us to prove we are no longer in love? How many summers and Septembers, distractions and chance meetings, remnants of our sad, hopeful love in another's look, an all too familiar gesture— how long do we go on dragging our aching bodies day after day through this yawning, yearning world, searching for a glimpse of what could have been?

Tell me there has been someone else like me, for you. That your experience of love has not been defined by the way I spoke your name into the hollow of your neck. Ask me if I have found the same kind of reverence anywhere else but in your slow, patient hands, your sea-salt lips spilling laughter mid-sentence, my heart rising in a crescendo like a wave ready to crash.

As you whispered to me, *love is the only thing that time cannot touch*.

After all this time, my love for you burns constant and true, my guiding light, my morning star. Time is testament to the relentless, unyielding power of this old, ancient love. A love I will carry with me, from eons to oceans to inches, back to you.

My Life

I will celebrate this life of mine, with or without you. The moon does not need the sun to tell her she is already whole.

From a Dream

There are three stages of waking:

Remembering who you are.
Forgetting what you dreamt.
Letting go of what you felt in that dream.

Sometimes they happen like waves, one after another. At times they can occur in no particular order. Other times they overlap all at once.

That's what it was like to love you. It was like waking from a dream.

When It's Over

There is a point in every relationship when you realize it's over and seldom is it the day you break up. For some, that moment is long after you say goodbye. For others, the moment is long before.

Once in Love

I don't think you need to be in love to write. But you had to have been once.

Thirty-Three Locks

It's almost ten years
        since I arrived here,
        to this idle, halcyon town,
        this little seaside house.

There are six doors
        and fourteen windows.
        There are thirty-three locks.
        I turn them over in my head
        when I can't sleep at night.
        I get out of bed to
        press my face against
        the tempered glass.

Once, I lived in a room
        without a window.
        I bet you could still see
        the places I wore the paint
        thin with my fingernails.
        I still think about it sometimes.
        Some nights my mind
        feels just like that room.

Left Too Late

Remember that old clock in our hall;
    how it chimed on the hour.

How my watch was set to yours—
    when time was worth keeping.

Before you said to me—you said,
    You're always too late or leaving.

Love Hurts

Do you remember what you said to me that day, long before
we knew what we would be, before you whispered my name
to me, raw and tender, like it hurt you to say it?

You told me you were the bravest when you're in love, so
don't you dare stand there and tell me you're afraid.

Sandcastles

The roar of the ocean
    like an endless echo,
    of that postcard afternoon;
    when I heard your laughter
    like a storm rolling in the distance.

If love had a scent, it would
    be seaweed and sandcastles,
    on the cusp of November,
    and the sigh of your breath
    on my sun-kissed skin.

The memory of you like a
    loaded gun in my hand—
    my finger on the trigger.

The One Thing

Look at you. You've stitched your life so perfectly together. You worked so damn hard to get to where you are, and now have everything you ever wanted. So why do you keep looking back at the one thing that can undo it all?

Wishing Well

Into a well
a girl threw a penny.

What do you wish for?
asked the well.
I wish for a penny,
said the girl.

Danger of Love

Let's live this life half-lived,
    and dare not hope for more;
    not a single thought we'll give—
    to the one, we loved most of all.

Let's love with hearts half-hearted—
    and walk through life asleep.
    Do not dream of dreams departed,
    of the one, we couldn't keep.

Let's not look for silver linings,
    or send our wishes to the stars;
    for there is danger in our pining,
    and we are safer where we are.

A New Day

I shed my past like layers of skin. I let them fall at my feet like discarded clothing.

I pay my dues and make amends for the sins of my youth. I step out from the shadows and into the light, naked and free.

I can hear my spirit singing. I can feel my wings unfolding.

And the sky is calling my name.

From You

The distance from you is measured in how far I've come.

Smoke & Mirrors

If you know she's too good for you. If she makes you think about the universe. If you look into her eyes and see the best version of yourself reflected back—

why do you hesitate?

If you feel the joy of possibility coursing through your veins. If she makes you feel more alive than you've ever felt. If she opens up a whole new world for you—

why would you let that tempt you?

I know you're young and there is so much life left in you. But deep down, you know she is the one. It's true the world is a great big place, and you're not done exploring every inch of it. But, sweetheart, it's all just smoke and mirrors.

And if you don't make her yours now, someone else will.

And you're going to regret it for the rest of your life.

Pretense

The greatest injustice I have suffered has come under the pretense of love.

About Love

When I was five I asked my mother about love. She scooped me into her arms and spun me around, her laughter filling up the room. She said love was like a red, round balloon; there was a part of you that wanted to hold on to it, a part of you that longed to see it soar into the big, open sky.

At ten, I asked my mother again about love. A soft smile played on her lips when she said love was like a drowsy kitten that came to you, unbidden, crawled into your lap, and made you the center of its world.

The day I turned twenty, I dared to ask my mother one last time about love. She tucked a lock of my hair behind my ear and held my young, hopeful face between her gentle hands. Her eyes were raw with longing when she answered, *love is a dormant volcano, lying in wait, biding its time.*

Thoughts on Letting Go

It's possible to move on from someone even if your heart refuses to let go. And it's not something you need to consciously do. It will just happen gradually, over time. The ache will always be there, but the intensity will fade, and you'll find other beautiful things to fill your days with.

Two Worlds

I try to imagine how your name would sound in my mother tongue, like the phantom words that exist only in the language I was born to, that if said out loud would seem to you, incomprehensible.

How do I tell you when my words are a patchwork of two worlds that fit so beautifully in my mind but become unstuck, like pieces of a puzzle, the moment they fall from my lips?

What I feel for you is at once the expression of language and the absence of it.

All the Time

Did you find your ever after?
    Is there somewhere you belong?
    Is your world now filled with laughter?
    Is there nothing for which you long?

Do you ever look behind you?
    And wonder about what you see?
    When the memories come to find you—
    do you ever think of me?

Do you think that love can lessen,
    if you pretend it isn't there?
    Do you ever, ever question,
    what could have been if we dared?

Are you happy to let it linger?
    Does it never cross your mind?
    The world that slipped through our fingers—
    I think of it all the time.

To Myself, Ten Years Ago

You won't believe what I see from this vantage point, the years stretching out before you like a long and winding road. I don't want to scare you, but there is a forest just up ahead. One so dense and dark, the sunlight won't reach you for awhile. You will wander lost, in this long, perilous night, not knowing if it will ever come to an end. But believe me, the light will find you again, and when it does, you will no longer be afraid of the dark.

Stop to catch your breath. Soon, a jagged mountain will rise before you, so steep it will make you want to turn back around. Don't despair; the first foothold is always the most difficult and every inch you claim of that cold, hard precipice will make you stronger. Before you know it, the ground will level out beneath you, and you will look back to see you had conquered what you once thought impossible.

See that turn just up ahead? That's the place where love will meet you, with arms so warm it will melt away the winter in an instant. And then, it will be summer for a very long time.

Over

It's over, she said.

It was many years later when the quiet realization dawned on her.

It's over, her heart whispered.

Back to Life

I want to wrap my mouth
    around yours, like a word
    that sits on the tip of my tongue,
    one I can't wait to say out loud.

I want to throw your name
    from the edge of a cliff
    and lose it in the great abyss,
    to feel it swelling up like a tide
    in my mouth all over again.

I want you to spill from my lips
    like a rupture of joy, like a deluge
    of rain across the weathered
    landscape of my soul, a rushing river
    that carries me back to love,
    brings me back to life.

Poetry and Prose

Sometimes I am caught between poetry and prose, like two lovers I can't decide between.

Prose says to me, let's build something long and lasting.

Poetry takes me by the hand, and whispers,

come with me, let's get lost for awhile.

Goddess

Have you forgotten who you are? Here is a reminder. You are the giver of light, of life.

Do you have any idea of your power?

Every time your body bends,

the universe yields to you.

Your eyes are twin worlds they send up satellites to orbit. And your skin

is made up of the very fabric of time.

Look for the light within you. Feel it surge like a river through your veins.

Use it to will your dreams into existence.

After All

I felt you again in my sleep last night. Like always my dreams of you are peripheral. An overheard conversation where your name is mentioned; a letter in my hand I try desperately to read before I wake. A Styrofoam coffee cup and half-read book on an empty table where I knew you were just minutes before. It's as though my dreams are a mirror of my waking world, like finding myself walking down the street where I could have sworn I caught a glimpse of you, only to look again and realize it wasn't you after all.

Call to Action

Do you hear the angry winds bellowing?
    The light from a single torch is burning;
    the sea that roars onto the shoreline,
    tells us that the tide is turning.

Do you feel the blood within you flowing?
    From rivers to oceans—here we stand;
    this is the time of our deliverance,
    the power we now hold in hand.

Do you see the flicker of light now growing?
    A wildfire roars in Liberty's name;
    the seraphic flame of our Awakening,
    it is now our time to rise again.

The Mermaid

Sometimes you wonder about her. That girl who is so much like a mermaid. Who lives in the depths of the ocean, separate from the real world. You don't hear from her for years at a time. And that's when you know she is happy. She only comes back to the surface out of loneliness or necessity.

More to Me

What never was,
    What could have been,
    was more to me
    than anything else.

A Dream of Hope

Last night I slept for the first time since
    you left and I dreamt about two suns
    in an apocalyptic sky, one edged in
    black and smoldering, like a cigarette burn.

I saw the sea rise up so high outside
    the window of my mother's old house
    so I climbed up onto the tin roof
    to look inside the mouth of Neptune.

In a hotel room where we couldn't figure
    out the light switches, my legs were
    wrapped around you and I was humming
    a tune that we both knew by heart.

There was a woman who made a shrine
    for her dead lover in the hollow of a tree.
    She looked straight at me with eyes
    milky white and whispered, *it's not too late.*

Letter by Letter

Sometimes it feels like my pen is another vessel, another vein, organic like the blood that rushes through, and spills onto paper. And my heart, tired and tender, beats out your name, letter by letter. While my mind, a thousand miles a minute, tries to take it all back.

Revenge

When the battle is done,
    and you think you have won—
    don't dance on my grave just yet.

If you are the moon,
    then I am the sun—
    I will not allow you to forget.

In my own time
    I will take back what's mine,
    for I am not your friend.

In the dark of the night,
    And the shifting of tides—
    I will come for you then.

Too Far In

I look for you, the way I was taught to look both ways when crossing the road. Uptight and wary, bracing myself for something I know could break me.

I loved you, in the way I'd only known love. Before I learned to hold back. When I thought everyone loved with their eyes closed and hearts wide open.

After you, I learned to lock my doors at night, pull the curtain shut. Be wary of strangers with taut arms and sad eyes. Who want to spill their secrets to you like the ocean, who pull back once you find yourself too far in.

I miss you, like a drowsy child begging for sleep; like a bird who almost made it to the sun. I ache for you like the searing memory of flight.

To Us

What has time done to us? It has turned my body into yearning. It has made you so much more powerful, more intoxicating than flesh and bone.

Borrowed Love

Kiss him if you want to;
    you are treading on
    sacred ground.
    Anywhere you go,
    I have already been.
    And when you put your body
    next to his,
    you'll find the places
    I mapped out long before
    he knew you.

And when he calls your name,
    know I was the one
    who put up those walls.
    You should know by now
    that you cannot build
    cities on cities.

Kiss him if you want to;
    But keep this in mind—
    you are a tourist here.
    I was his first love
    and I'll be his last.

Crazy Love

Anyone who knew me then would say I loved you far too much. Like a wildfire or the sharp edge of a knife.

Anyone would have told you I stopped being the person I was the second you walked into my life.

They would have said love wasn't supposed to drive you crazy, make you want to scratch at your skin.

And they were right.

Because there was love and then there was you.

The Irony of Love

The closer I get to love, the further away it seems.

To Know

To know that I miss you,
    so much when you leave.
    To know that I need you
    like the air that I breathe.

To know that I want you,
    with a passion so blind.
    Is to know that I love you,
    with no doubt in my mind.

All This Love

I don't know where it comes from, all this love I have for you. I don't know where to put it now that you're gone.

Who You Love

The life you always thought you wanted before you knew any different. The sea change you didn't see coming, the sweeping vistas and cotton candy sunsets.

The meeting point between how you imagined it would be and how it has transpired. The willingness to take a chance on something that could take you somewhere new.

The dream you chose to give up on, or the one that you were coaxed into following.

Who you love and who loves you back determines so much in your life.

When I'm Happy

That's the thing about happiness. It doesn't require justifica-
tion. When I'm happy, I'm happy. I don't feel the need to
write about it.

Writers & Poets

We live in a world where writing ages like wine. Sometimes it takes years or even centuries to mature.

But if history has shown us one thing, it is the merit of writers who spoke the language of the people; who have taken poetry out of the shadows and into the light.

Writers and poets who are ahead of their time.

They are the ones whose works will endure.

The Nature of Love

If I could tell my younger self one thing, it would be this:

There are many things in life you can postpone, but love isn't one of them.

Bloom

Someone once planted your name
  like a seed in my heart.

Only now I've met you,
  do I know what it means to bloom.

Transcript of Your Heart

If there is someone else for you now, then why do you linger here? We've said our goodbyes, but your eyes won't let me go. I can see it on your face, everything you have ever felt for me. My name is still written there, a trail in permanent ink, a transcript of your heart.

Strings

Some people are made like the string of a kite, loose and free, like a bird riding the wind. Some people are made like the hard, brittle rope of a mountaineer, strong, steady, infallible. And then there are the ones who are like the strings of a violin, delicate and ethereal. Strung tight and taut, ready to snap. But when they sing, there is no other sound more haunting or beautiful.

Our Love

This is where our love is found,
    in a strange little rhyme;
    where in space the beat of our hearts resound,
    while our bones lie in the ground.

Little fragments ground down with time,
    where fingers once were intertwined,
    and I wore your ring, and you wore mine.

To Love You

It feels bittersweet to love you, as though time has already run its ruinous path and everything good is over before it begins.

It feels perilous to love you, like a dust storm swallowing up the sky or a comet skimming the stratosphere.

But it is an honor to love you. I will love you for as long as I can.

Twice As Much

I have mourned you every day,
    for every picture torn from my shelf.
    Since the wind had carried you away,
    I find I think of little else.

I have mourned the words we spoke,
    the mouth you pressed into my back;
    the autumn leaves that fell and fell—
    and left a girl in winter black.

All these years—still I can't forget,
    the face my hands no longer touch.
    And the wretched day you leave this world—
    I will mourn you twice as much.

Love What You Love

Love what you love with reckless abandon.
Share the things that mirror your soul.
Let those who undermine you
shed light on their own self-doubt.
Glow with the pride of your assertions.

Anticipation

There is a stirring in my soul, a restless, wild anticipation. I am staring out into the horizon, as far as I can. I can't see what's beyond it, but I can feel it.

Be the One

You couldn't be the one—the one to love her.

She dazzled you, but your eyes could never get used to the light. So you remained clothed in shadow, and ignored the hand that reached for you.

You ignored your own heart.

And that is why you couldn't be the one.

She wasn't just the moon; she was the whole sky, but you couldn't see beyond the stratosphere.

Your souls loved each other as much as any two souls could possibly love—

but you couldn't be the one.

Whole Again

I have moved so far away from you that I have become a myth; a lie you tell yourself each night. I am the one true thing you've held in the palm of your hand, the key to everything you wanted.

Your name smiles at me from a crumpled envelope, addressed to the past. Unsent and unseen. Inside I wrote you a story about the moon, how night after night the darkness carved at the pale curve of her body until she became half the woman she was.

There is a word that hurts my heart—one I don't ever say out loud. Like the shadow that lingers in the light, I can't separate myself from your memory. But there are some nights when I look up at the sky, and the moon is whole again.

No Longer Mine

It should be my right to mourn someone who has yet to leave this world but no longer wants to be part of mine.

Misunderstood

Today I feel small—looked down on and disregarded. My thoughts are of little importance. My words have no bearing on the weight of the world. I am tired of being taken for granted. If only I could get back a fraction of what I give. But my efforts go unnoticed, and my soul keeps wishing to be noticed, to be valued; to be understood.

To Dare

Spread your wings—now is the time,
    to dare, to dream, to reach for the sky.
    This is the moment you will soar;
    if you want it now—you can have it all.

Others will look upon your grace,
    and their bitter hearts will cry in spite;
    the best parts of you—they'll try to take,
    to dim the brilliance of your light.

And as your tender courage wanes,
    something whispers to you—wait!
    Look them in the eye and say—not today,
    I will not let you guide my fate.

This is not the day when you'll concede,
    you have more strength than you could know.
    This is when you will—if you believe,
    show them just how far you'll go.

Here and Now

Here and now I love you,
> for the moment you have my heart.
> But you are not entitled to my future,
> you have no ownership of my past.

Writer's Block

Lately I have been wishing there was more time to write. That everything would stop spinning for just a moment so I could sit down and tap blissfully away. Like I used to.

Today I saw two strangers sitting side by side at a park bench, their fingers just inches from each other. Both were silent, staring straight ahead and neither seemed in any particular hurry to leave.

On my walk home, I wondered who they were and what destiny had in store for them. Will they remain strangers or become friends—perhaps even lovers?

Then a thought occurred to me. While I am trying to find time to write, while my words are gathering dust in some sort of cosmic inventory—life is giving me a story.

Ad Infinitum

The solution
    is neither
    further nor nearer.

Like the mirror
    of a mirror
    of a mirror.

For Yours

You were the one who taught her strength and humility in equal parts. You were the one who lifted her up, brought her down to her knees. And now here she is, the girl who has never had to ask for anyone's love, asking for yours.

A Letter to My Love

Remember what we spoke about all those years ago. We said we'd run away and live in the South of France, just the two of us and the ocean. It hasn't happened like how we pictured, but it is exactly how it was always meant to be.

You, me, and the sea.

You know, I've never been sentimental. I shy away from it in our day to day. But building this life with you has been the grandest adventure. It feels like I am living it simultaneously in the present and the far-off future, sifting through my memories. I am already nostalgic for what we have, even with you still here.

This is the happiest I have ever been. The most at peace with myself and all things that anchor me to this world. I have grown with our love, it is a place of shelter. My island of solace. With you, I have seen all my dreams come into fruition. Everything I want is here in this moment. All I ask now is for time with you, as much as we are allowed.

Closer to Me

It was long ago, yet you feel closer to me than yesterday, more hopeful than tomorrow.

You are as far and near as memory.

As distant as the sun,

as close as its light on my skin.

Every Feeling

There was a time when I felt everything there was to feel with you. From blinding rage to bitter jealousy; searing love to utter despair. And then, the worst one of all—sweet, irrational hope—like a hypnotic melody leading me to the edge of a cliff.

Here I am on the other side, the baptism of every human emotion. What happens after you feel everything there is to feel? Somehow, there is a sense of comfort in knowing nothing will ever hit me quite as hard again. Nothing will ever be as beautiful, but neither will anything hurt as much.

Love Poetry

What we once knew as conversation,
　　we now know as poetry.

When once we made love with our words,
　　we now make words with our love.

The Girl You Once Had

You put too much faith in my love for you, but, honey, I was stronger than anything you could have imagined. The biggest mistake you made was thinking I would stay exactly where you left me. Now I've gone so far, so fast, you'll never get close enough to hurt me again. The girl you once had in the palm of your hand is now holding all the cards.

How Much Love

How much love is a person capable of giving? I thought I knew the answer until I met you.

One of Them

In any given day,
a million people
will skim their eyes
over my words.

Sometimes I wonder
if you're one of them.

We the Poets

Where they destroy, we create;
where they criticize, we inspire.
That is why they are the critics,
and we are the poets.

How It Ends

Imagine if you had a moment with your past self. Revealed to them, your entire history with me, before our paths were set to cross.

Our whole love story mapped out, like a book, where neither of us can change the outcome.

If you had the choice, would you go through it again with me? Despite knowing how it ends, would you still want to love me?

Index

Acknowledgments

Thank you to my agent, Al Zuckerman; Samantha; and the team at Writers House for your encouragement and support.

To Kirsty, Patty, and the team at Andrews McMeel for taking a chance on poetry all those years ago. What an incredible journey it has been!

To Michael and Ollie for all the wonderful memories we've shared in our little house by the sea. I look forward to many more.

To the talented artist gg, thank you for lending your gorgeous work to the cover of this book.

To my beautiful readers—there are no words to describe how much you mean to me. Thank you a million times over.

About the Author

Lang Leav is an international bestselling author of four poetry and prose books. She is the winner of a Qantas Spirit of Youth Award, Churchill Fellowship, and Goodreads Choice Award. Her debut novel, *Sad Girls*, continues to top bestseller charts worldwide.

Lang has been featured in various publications, including the *Sydney Morning Herald*, the *Straits Times*, the *Guardian*, and the *New York Times*. She currently resides in New Zealand with her partner and fellow author Michael Faudet.

Join Lang Leav on the following:

Facebook   Tumblr   Twitter   Instagram